# EXPLORING WORLD CULTURES

# Pakistan

Kate Shoup

## Cavendish Square

New York

Published in 2019 by Cavendish Square Publishing, LLC
243 5th Avenue, Suite 136, New York, NY 10016

Copyright © 2019 by Cavendish Square Publishing, LLC

First Edition

Library of Congress Cataloging-in-Publication Data

Names: Shoup, Kate, 1972- author.
Title: Pakistan / Kate Shoup.
Description: First edition. | New York : Cavendish Square, 2019. | Series: Exploring world cultures | Includes index. | Audience: Grades 2-5.
Identifiers: LCCN 2017048027 (print) | LCCN 2017051366 (ebook) | ISBN 9781502638069 (library bound) | ISBN 9781502638076 (paperback) | ISBN 9781502638083 (6 pack) | ISBN 9781502638090 (ebook)
Subjects: LCSH: Pakistan--Juvenile literature.
Classification: LCC DS376.9 (ebook) | LCC DS376.9 .S56 2018 (print) | DDC 954.91--dc23
LC record available at https://lccn.loc.gov/2017048027

Editorial Director: David McNamara
Editor: Jodyanne Benson
Copy Editor: Rebecca Rohan
Associate Art Director: Amy Greenan
Designer: Christina Shults
Production Coordinator: Karol Szymczuk
Photo Research: J8 Media

Printed in the United States of America

# Contents

# Introduction

The Islamic Republic of Pakistan was created in 1947. Pakistan used to be part of India. Now India and Pakistan are two different countries. Pakistan is the name for five regions in India that became part of Pakistan. They are called Punjab, Afghania, Kashmir, Sindh, and Baluchistan. Pakistan means "land of the pure" in the Urdu and Persian languages.

People from Pakistan call themselves Pakistanis. Nearly all Pakistanis follow the Islam religion. People who are part of this religion are called Muslims. Muslims believe in a god called Allah and a prophet named Muhammad.

Although most Pakistanis are Muslim, they are not all the same. There are many different ethnic groups in Pakistan. Ethnic groups celebrate similar language and culture.

There are many beautiful places here. Some of the world's tallest mountains are here. Pakistan also has deserts, farmland, and seashores. Many types of plants and animals live in Pakistan.

Pakistan is a special country. There is a lot to learn about the culture.

# Geography

Pakistan is in South Asia. It covers 340,509 square miles (881,913 square kilometers). Pakistan shares land borders with Afghanistan, China, India, and Iran. It also borders the Arabian Sea. There are

This map shows the regions in Pakistan.

fourteen mountain ranges in Pakistan. One famous mountain range is the Himalayas. Pakistan's tallest

## FACT!

The Indus River is the longest river in Pakistan. It starts in Western Tibet and flows all the way to the Arabian Sea. The Indus River is the national river of Pakistan.

## Seasons

Pakistan has four seasons. Winter is cold in the mountains. Summer is **monsoon** season.

mountain is K2. It is the second-highest peak in the world. It is 28,251 feet (8,611 meters) tall.

There is a desert in Pakistan. It is called the Thar Desert. South of this desert is the Indus Plain. There are many farms there.

K2 is the second-highest peak in the world.

Pakistan has many types of animals. Leopards, hyenas, bears, and crocodiles live in Pakistan. Pakistan also has more than 650 types of birds.

People have lived in South Asia for thousands of years. In fact, this area was home to one of the first civilizations on Earth: the Indus Valley Civilization. It lasted for 2,000 years. After that, it broke into several parts. Each part had its own leader.

These ruins from the Indus Valley Civilization were discovered in 1922.

During the 1800s, Britain took over the area. In 1947, the British government gave it up. The area was split into two countries: India and Pakistan. India was given to the Hindus and Sikhs in the area. Pakistan was given to the Muslims.

This caused a huge **migration**. Muslims moved from India to Pakistan. Hindus and Sikhs moved from Pakistan to India.

Mohammed Ali Jinnah was Pakistan's first governor-general.

## Pakistan's First Leader

Mohammed Ali Jinnah was the founder of Pakistan. He worked to protect Muslims when Pakistan was controlled by Britain as part of India.

9

VOTE ✓

The Islamic Republic of Pakistan is made up of four provinces and four territories. A central government oversees these provinces and territories. In addition, each province has its own local government.

Pakistan's Parliament House is located in the city of Islamabad.

The central government is a parliamentary republic. It has three branches:

- Legislative: This branch is called parliament. The parliament of Pakistan is divided into two groups. Members of both groups write new laws.
- Judicial: This branch is made up of the courts. It follows the country's constitution.

There are 442 members of parliament. They are elected. They meet at Parliament House in Islamabad. Islamabad is the capital of Pakistan.

- Executive: The president and the prime minister make up this branch of government. The prime minister is the head of government.

Today, Pakistan is a democracy. This was not always the case. For many years, the country was ruled by its military.

A Pakistani woman casts her vote.

## Voting

All Pakistani citizens who are eighteen and older can vote in elections. In some areas of Pakistan, it is still very difficult for women to vote.

# The Economy

It used to be that most Pakistanis were farmers. They grew crops such as wheat, sugarcane, cotton, and rice. Now, more Pakistanis work in the service industry. For example, they work as teachers, doctors, or bus drivers. The service industry makes up more than half of Pakistan's **gross domestic product (GDP)**.

A Pakistani woman picks cotton on a farm. Pakistan grows a lot of cotton.

FACT!

Many tourists come to Pakistan to climb its tall mountains. These tourists help boost the local economy.

12

A country's GDP measures how well the economy is doing. Other Pakistanis work in factories. Some of these factories make clothing. Other factories make cement, steel, and machines.

Pakistan is a developing country. This means there is less industry than in some other countries. However, the country's economy is growing fast. In fact, Pakistan could soon become one of the world's largest economies.

These bills are examples of Pakistani money.

## Money

Money in Pakistan is called the Pakistani rupee. One rupee equals about one US penny.

# The Environment

A growing economy is good because it helps people out of poverty. But it is often bad because it creates environmental problems. This is true in Pakistan.

Some cities in Pakistan have dirty air.

One environmental problem in Pakistan is dirty air. Dirty air makes it difficult for people to breathe. It is caused by cars, factories, and the burning of garbage.

## FACT!

Experts warn that Pakistan will likely have more floods and droughts because of climate change.

Another environmental problem is dirty water. Dirty water spreads disease. It is caused by dumping sewage into rivers and lakes.

A third environmental problem is **deforestation**. This is the cutting down of trees to make room for farms or to produce paper or wood products. Deforestation is harmful to plants and animals.

Deforestation is a problem in Pakistan.

## Protecting the Environment

The government of Pakistan is working to fix environmental problems. One way it does so is by teaching the importance of conservation, community spirit, and responsibility within Islam.

Pakistan is the sixth-most-populated country on Earth. More than 201 million people live in Pakistan.

A group of Pakistani children celebrate Independence Day.

Pakistan has six main ethnic groups. The largest is the Punjabi group. Punjabis make up more than 46 percent of Pakistan's population.

## FACT!

By 2030, Pakistan will likely be the most populous Muslim country in the world.

More than half of all Pakistanis are less than thirty years old. Of these, roughly 70 percent are younger than fifteen. On average, Pakistani men live sixty-five years. Pakistani women live sixty-seven years.

Around seven million Pakistanis live in other countries. Many send money to their families in Pakistan.

## Refugees

Millions of **refugees** live in Pakistan. Many are from Afghanistan. Afghanistan has been at war for more than thirty years. First, it fought against the Union of Soviet Socialist Republics. Then, it fought against the United States of America.

# Lifestyle

Half the people in Pakistan live in large towns or cities. The other half live in the countryside. Most country dwellers live off the land. Often, their homes lack electricity and running water. City life is more modern.

Karachi is a very busy city in Pakistan.

Family is important to Pakistanis. Several family members might live together in one house. Most Pakistani families are **patriarchal**. That means the men are in charge. Arranged marriages are common. In an arranged marriage, a person's family chooses his or her mate.

Karachi is the largest city in Pakistan. More than twenty-four million people live there.

Pakistani girls and women do not have the same rights as men. Many become victims of violence. One victim was Malala Yousafzai. She was shot on her way home from school for speaking up for women's rights.

Malala Yousafzai stood up against violence.

## Malala Yousafzai's Inspiration

Malala Yousafzai was inspired by a Pakistani woman named Benazir Bhutto. Bhutto twice served as the country's prime minister. Sadly, Bhutto was killed in 2008.

19

# Religion

The official religion of Pakistan is Islam. In fact, Pakistan was created for Muslims. More than 96 percent of all Pakistanis are Muslim. Most Pakistanis are Sunni Muslims.

This group of Muslims is praying in a mosque.

Islam is an important part of Pakistani culture. It is the basis for many laws. These laws are very strict. Pakistan

## FACT!

One **sect**, or group, of Muslims is the Sunni Muslims. Another is the Shia Muslims. Because of their differences, members of these two sects often do not get along.

does not promote religious freedom. This makes life difficult for the small number of Pakistanis who are not Muslim.

Muslims worship in special buildings called mosques. There are many beautiful mosques in Pakistan. One is called the Mohabbat Khan Mosque. It is located in the city of Peshawar.

The Mohabbat Khan Mosque is a beautiful mosque in Pakistan.

## Islam

Muslims refer to God as Allah. They believe a man named Muhammad was a prophet. A holy book called the Quran describes Allah and Muhammad and lists the rules of Islam.

# Language

Pakistan has more than seventy languages. Many of these are regional languages. This means they are spoken only in certain parts of the country. One regional language is Punjabi. It is spoken in the Punjab region

## Urdu Alphabet

Urdu uses different letters than English.

of Pakistan. Another is Sindhi. It is spoken in the Sindh province. Each language has its own books, poems, songs, and sayings.

Pakistan has two official languages. One is Urdu. It is similar to Hindi. Hindi is spoken by most people in neighboring India. The other language is English. English is often used in business and government.

Many Pakistanis speak more than one language. For example, they might speak a regional language, Urdu, and English.

## Urdu

Urdu uses different letters than English. There are thirty-eight letters in all. These letters are written from right to left.

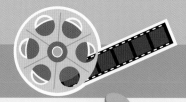

Pakistanis listen to many types of music. They like pop, rock, disco, and folk music. Pakistan also makes its own movies. The actors speak Urdu. Many Pakistani movies are made in the city of Lahore. These are called Lollywood films. Others are made in Karachi. These are called Kariwood films.

Pakistanis celebrate at a festival in Kalash.

Television is even more popular than movies. Pakistanis like dramas and miniseries.

Pakistan has many festivals and holidays. Most of these have to do with Islam. One is

Ramadan. It lasts for a whole month. Another is Eid-al-Fitr. It is the last day of Ramadan. A third is Eid-al-Adha. On this day, Muslims share food with friends, family, and the poor.

## Ramadan

Ramadan celebrates the prophet Muhammad's first reading of the Quran. During Ramadan, Muslims **fast** each day from sunrise to sunset.

Pakistan has a national sport. It is field hockey. Field hockey was invented in Europe during the middle ages. Field hockey is like ice hockey, but players run instead of skate. Pakistan has won three Olympic gold medals in men's field hockey.

Cricket is the most popular sport in Pakistan.

## FACT!

Pakistan's national cricket team is called the Cornered Tigers. In 1992, Pakistan won the Cricket World Cup.

The most popular sport in Pakistan is cricket. It was invented in England in the middle ages. Cricket is like baseball. There is a bowler who pitches the ball, a batsman, and fielders. Pakistanis also enjoy polo and squash.

Pakistanis also play sports that were invented in South Asia. One is kho kho. It is like tag. Another is kabaddi. It is also like tag, but you play it while holding your breath.

Pakistani children play kabaddi together.

## Athletics

Pakistani athletes compete in the Islamic Solidarity Games. These are like the Olympic Games, but they are for Muslim countries.

# Food

Pakistanis eat lots of different kinds of food. Dishes served in one part of Pakistan might be very different from dishes in another part.

Kebab is a common food in Pakistan. It is meat cooked on a long stick.

One common food all over Pakistan is kebab. Kebab is grilled meat on a stick. Another common food is biryani. It has rice, meat, and spices. Pakistanis also enjoy curry. Many meals include rice, lentils, and a special kind of bread called naan.

## FACT!

In Pakistan, it is bad manners to eat with your left hand.

# Food and Drink

Certain food and drinks are not allowed by Islam. For example, Muslims cannot eat pork and cannot drink alcohol.

Pakistanis eat three meals each day (except during Ramadan). The main meal is dinner. Often, dinner is served with tea. After dinner, they eat dessert. One popular dessert is *gajar ka halwa*.

Pakistanis love to share a delicious meal together.

It is made from carrots. Another is *gulab jamun*. It contains fruit and rose water. Pakistanis also enjoy ice cream and bread pudding.

# Glossary

**deforestation**    The clearing away of trees for land to be used another way.

**fast**    To go without food or drink.

**gross domestic product (GDP)**    A measure of how a country's economy is doing.

**migration**    A movement from one area to another area.

**monsoon**    A special wind that often brings rain.

**patriarchal**    Describes a society in which men are in charge.

**refugees**    People who are forced to leave their country because of war, bad government, or natural disasters.

**sect**    A religious group.

# Find Out More

## Books

Doak, Robin S. *Malala Yousafzai*. London: C. Press/F. Watts Trade, 2015

Sonneborn, Liz. *Pakistan*. New York: Scholastic, 2012.

## Website

**Britannica Kids: Pakistan**

http://kids.britannica.com/kids/article/

Pakistan/345761

## Video

**15 Interesting Facts About Pakistan You Should Know**

https://www.youtube.com/watch?v=GRQxrE-ONIQ

# Index

# About the Author

**Kate Shoup** has written more than forty books and has edited hundreds more. When not working, Kate, an IndyCar fanatic, loves to ski, read, and ride her motorcycle. She lives in Indianapolis with her husband, her daughter, and their dog.